D0006951

Further Still

Further Still

A collection of poetry and vignettes

BETH MOORE

BROADMAN
&HOLMAN
PUBLISHERS

Nashville, Tennessee

Published by Broadman & Holman Publishers,
Nashville, Tennessee

ISBN 0-8054-3093-8

Dewey Decimal Classification: 248.84
Subject Heading: CHRISTIAN LIFE—POETRY

Unless otherwise noted, Scripture quotations are from
the Holy Bible, New International Version, copyright
© 1973, 1978, 1984 by International Bible Society. Also
used is the King James Version.

1 2 3 4 5 6 7 8 9 10 09 08 07 06 05 04

To my Dad, a true servant of God,
and Maddy, the most wonderful
stepmom in the world

I love you both,
Beth

Contents

Moving On   1

Further Still   7

Childhood   9

Immanuel   12

Lullaby   14

Birth of the King   15

Little One   19

Chosen in Tarsus   20

Side by Side   25

Watercolor Mister   28

Holding Us   29

Amanda   30

Twilight Wishes   31

Shadow   33

I May Never Walk on Water   36

My Name Is Pride   37

Had   39

A Healing Captive   42

Nanny's Box   44

Come, Captive, Free!   52

A Tattletale   54

Fellowship   55

Sitting Long   57
Audience of One   58
The River of Mercy   63
The Streets of Jerusalem   64
River of Delights   66
Fragile   67
The Sinner's Prayer   68
Blessed Anonymity   71
An Unfamiliar Place   72

Service   75

Who Is This?   78
A House that Grace Built   82
Unlovely   85
Drink Offering   86
Your People   87
Need Me   89
Lord, Make Me a Student   94
Lesson with a Hairbrush   95
Think Bigger, Boys   106
Commission to Faith   108

The Road Home   111

My Prodigal   114
Elohim   115
Consume Me, O Lord   118

Footsteps to Follow   120
The Apple of Your Eye   121
Wedding Portrait   123
Blessed Condescension   130
The Poet   132
John, the Beloved   133
What Kind of God Are You?   138
Shining like the Son   139

Resources   147

MOVING ON

Along this path of ministry, God has used an approach over and over again that I've finally come to more readily expect. He has taught me to listen to the repetitive requests of the body of Christ, and I will often discover what He wants me to do. Case in point: I had no plan whatsoever to write women's Bible studies. In fact, I was quite content teaching Sunday school, speaking at conferences, and teaching an interdenominational weekday class. The latter gave me the time and opportunity to plunge deeper into the Word. I had no idea just how deep that particular class would insist we plunge.

After several years of giving weekly Bible lectures, several women in the class approached me and stated confidently, "We want you to start writing homework for us." To which I immediately responded with a more confident, "No way under heaven. I can't write homework." I then suggested several other Bible studies they could attend that provided excellent homework assignments. They persisted in annoying me half to death. I've written, let's see, about ten in-depth Bible studies since the day I finally caved in to the pressure.

Many of the major moves in my ministry have come the same way. In one way or another, God has used numbers of others to tell me through persistent requests what to do next. Certainly not every need or request constitutes a call, but sheer volume followed by God's apparent affirmation has been a tremendously helpful guide. The concept makes plenty of sense if you think about it. If spiritual gifts are given to edify the body of Christ, and Scripture clearly says they are, then God often uses that same body to tell us what it needs from us is reasonable.

This book certainly constitutes such an approach of God's leadership. Neither of the poetry/creative writing books, *Things Pondered* or *Further Still*, have been my idea. Frankly, others have needled me into them. I don't mind. In fact, I'm so humbled by it I hardly know what to do. The problem is that I can't figure out for the life of me why anyone would want these writings particularly since, in a volume like this, they aren't surrounded by the original environment they were written to reflect. We've all heard the term "location joke." You know the kind. The story falls flat. Your face turns crimson and you mutter, "Well, I guess you had to be there." I confess in advance that after every entry I fear I'll need to mutter the same. But what can I say? You asked for it! And, so, because serving you is the absolute joy of my earthly existence, I'm handing it over.

If you weren't one of those who asked for it, then I very likely could owe you an apology. Don't worry. Apologizing comes pretty easy for me. I've spent much of my ministry apologizing to people for what appears to be a rather odd show of taste on the part of the One who called me. I have no idea why in this world God has risked His name on someone like me. I will never comprehend such grace and stubbornness of will to teach a woman with a penchant for ditches how to walk a higher path. Jesus

Christ is the uncontested Champion of my life. He is the only good that dwells in me. I know He performs miracles because I am one. And if anything of my journey with Him could encourage you in yours, you are welcome to it.

So, welcome to this second volume of the ponderings (mutterings?) from a lesser woman. I want to thank my dear editor, Dale McCleskey, my friend Betsy Wedekind in Nashville, and the members of my staff who have contributed a special element to this volume. They collected many of the stories, poems, and passages that readers have requested. Thank you, beloved coworkers. Now when someone in the body of Christ asks for this or that reading out of one of the conferences or Bible studies, we will often be able to accommodate through one simple volume.

I invite you to join me in the pages to come as we reflect upon the glory of God and the wonder of everyday life with Him. Along the way we'll visit some scenes from the lives of biblical figures who have become a few of my best friends. Admittedly, I don't get out enough. Occasionally, I'll invite you to eavesdrop on the Moores. Since I consider you one of my best friends too, let's go as far as we can together, then at times I pray God will speak to you alone. You see, ultimately that's the destination of this book: further still. The name comes from a study God gave me based on Christ in the garden of Gethsemane. Allow a few passages from Matthew's Gospel to refresh your memory:

Then Jesus went with his disciples to a place called Gethsemane, and he said to them, "Sit here while I go over there and pray." He took Peter and the two sons of Zebedee along with him, and he began to be sorrowful and troubled. Then he said to them, "My soul is overwhelmed with sorrow to the point of death. Stay here and keep watch with me." Going a little farther, he fell with his face to the ground and prayed, "My Father, if it is possible, may this cup be taken from me. Yet not as I will, but as you will."

(Matt. 26:36–39)

Life can be almost unbearable at times, can't it? The one and only thing that has gotten me through my hardest times has been turning them into invitations to go further still with God. "Going a little further, . . . " With few exceptions, the writings in this volume that will seem the deepest were drawn from the well of pain. Sometimes our "further stills" come from the excruciating divine push to move from any hint of complacency into the brisk current of the river of God. I write this introduction to you on the second day of a new year. I just told God this morning that I want to keep going further with Him. I never want to grow stagnant or satisfied with my current knowledge of Christ. Beloved, there is so much more to Him and to the life He's given us than we have yet discovered. So, with that in mind, let's you and I go further still.

Further Still

In that lonely place
No friend can go
No brother can help
No loved one can know

I must crawl on
While you stay
Further Still
Just watch and pray

In that lonely place
The cup is fought
To sip the pain
Or choose my lot

To claim my rights
Or cast them down
To gain my loss
Or scorn my crown

Life pivots there
In Further Still
Face to the ground
Fighting His will

Can't choose to return
The same who went
Once Further Still
The old is spent

So remember me
And stay close by
I'll need you soon
Right by my side

And pray me back
Til He has won
And throat is parched
From "Yours be done!"

CHILDHOOD

I'm not sure God displays His wonder and creativity any more flamboyantly and miraculously than He does in a newborn baby. For that matter, a newborn anything. A few months ago, while in Kenya, I saw a newborn giraffe that caused me such joy I nearly threw my back out. For crying out loud, I even thought a baby warthog was cute. Nothing is like a newborn wrapped in human flesh, however. And if that's a miracle, what in the world would we call God wrapped in human flesh? We'd call it Immanuel, God with us.

While writing *Jesus, the One and Only*, I looked up the word *Immanuel* in the original language, and my heart was stirred by the structure of it. The *el* you see at the end of the name means "God," so if we were to take it literally in the order it was written, the name translates "the with of God." The thought prompted the following words.

Immanuel

Immanuel, the With of God
Incarnate Love on carnal sod.
Set aside Thy lofty crown
Knees of God kneeling down.
Spirit feet shod with flesh
Earth prints of celestial steps.
Fullness of the Deity
Draping God that man might see.
Volume of Thy silent voice
The Word made flesh—O, Blessed Choice!
What is man that Thou wouldst come
Wrapped as we, that we'd be one?
Wake, O Sleeper! Tongue must tell!
It's God with us!
Immanuel.

Imagine Gabriel searing earthward through the floor of the third heaven, breaking the barrier from the supernatural to the natural world. Feature him soaring through the second heaven past the stars God calls by name. As our vision "descends," the earth grows larger. God's kingdom gaze burns through the blue skies of planet Earth and plummets like a flaming stake in the ground to a backward town called Nazareth. (*Jesus, the Only and Only*, p. 9)

Lullaby

Hush, little baby, Daddy's got a Word
No eye has seen, no ear has heard.
Dream sweet dreams but you can't dream this
Plans your weaver weaves for bliss.

Hush, little baby, don't you cry
Daddy fixes all things by and by.
Cease your striving, rest your eyes
You're my joy and you're my prize.

Sleep, little baby, I'll stay awake
If skies should fall and mountains quake.
You'll be safe in Daddy's arms
Wrapped in blankets, robbed from harms.

Hush, little baby, I will sing
While angels dance and 'round you ring.
If I should come before you wake
Your eyes will open to Daddy's face.

So hush little baby, trust me now
Thrones and powers to me bow.
I tell oceans what to do
I think Daddy can take care of you.

Birth of the King

Picture that newborn with me. Beautiful dark eyes and skin, squirming in a young mother's inexperienced arms. "Hear" the sounds he makes. Gurgles. Coos. Hungry cries. The Savior of the world has come.

Her body lay sapped of strength, her eyes were heavily closed, but her mind refused to give way to rest. She ached for her mother. She wondered if she yet believed her. She heard the labored breathing of the man sleeping a few feet from her. Only months before he was little more than a stranger to her. She knew only what she had been told and what she could read in occasional shy glances. She had been told he was a good man. In the last days, she knew he was far more than a good man. No man, no matter how kind, could have done what he had done. She wondered how long it had been since he'd really rested. A calf, only a few days old, awakened hungry and could not find its mother. The stir awakened the baby who, too, squirmed to find his mother. Scarcely before she could move her tender frame toward the manger, he began to wail! She scooped him in her arms, her long hair draping his face, and she quietly slipped out of the gate. She sat down and leaned against the outside of the stable, propped the baby on her small lap, and taking a strip of linen and tying back her hair, she began to stare into his tiny face. She had not yet seen him in the light. She had never seen the moon so bright. The night was nearly as light as the day. Only hours old, his chin quivered, not from the cold, but from the sudden exposure of birth. His eyes were shaped like almonds and were as black as the deepest well. She held him tightly and quietly hummed a song she'd learned as a child. She had been so frightened of this moment, so sure she would not know what to do. She had never held an infant so small, and He was God, wrapped in soft, infant flesh, with bones so fragile she felt like He could break. She had pictured this moment so many times. What would the Son of the Spirit look like? She never expected him to look so normal, so common. Must have been the part he inherited from his mother. She was so sure she'd feel terribly awkward. So afraid she'd drop him, the Messiah, and God would be awfully sorry He had given Him to her! Instead, every fear, every doubt, every inadequacy was momentarily caught up in the indescribable rapture of a mother's affection.

She remembered asking Elizabeth things she dared not ask her dad and mother. Once when they were walking together at the end of the day, the wind blew her cousin's robes against her, and like a curious teenager, Mary tried her hardest to catch a good glimpse of Elizabeth's rounded middle. She herself had no physical evidence that God's promise was true. But she had enough faith to ask endless questions. What am I to do when He comes? Her cousin's reply would remain etched upon

Mary's heart long after He had saved the world. He will tell you what He needs from you. Beyond what He needs, all He wants is for you to embrace Him and talk to Him. She looked back in His delicate face and watched Him closely as He seemed to stare deeply into the moonlit sky. And she began to talk. Sweet baby boy. Do You know who Your Daddy is? Do You know Your name? Do You know why You're here? What do You see when You look out there? Can You see the stars? Do You remember their names? Do You think I'll do OK?

Will You love me too? A tear dropped from her chin to His. He yawned and made such a funny expression she grinned, wiping her face on the yellowed rags she'd draped around Him. The fussing calf had obviously found its mother. Not a sound was coming from inside the stable. The earth stilled. The infant slept. She held the babe next to her face, and for just a moment all the world silenced to the breath of God. She closed her eyes and listened, stealing time like a hidden metronome, as high and as wide as she dared to think, she still could not begin to comprehend. She, a common child of the most humble means who had never read the Scriptures for herself, was embracing the Incarnate Word. The fullness of the Godhead rested in her inexperienced arms, sleeping to the rhythm of her heart. This time she hummed a song she did not know, a song being sung by the choir of angels hovering over her head but hidden from her carnal senses. The deafening hallelujahs of the heavenly hosts were silent to mortal ears except through the sounds of a young woman's voice who had unknowingly given human notes to a holy score. The glory of God filled the earth. Heaven hammered a bridge, but one young woman sat completely unaware of all that swelled the atmosphere around her. The tiny baby boy had robbed her heart. "So this is what it feels like to be a mother," she mused. She crept back into the stable, wrapped Him in swaddling clothes, and laid Him in the manger. Just down the path, the sun peeked gently over the roof of an inn full of barren souls who had made Him no room.

Little One

Little One
Precious son
God must love you so . . .
Against all odds
A gift from God
For purposes He knows.
There's ball to play
Trucks to race
Motorcycles, too . . .
But most of all
Fulfill your call
God has chosen you.

Chosen in Tarsus

Just a few years after the birth of Jesus, another baby arrived. I find the thought of him tantalizing because he was born the son of a Pharisee . . . in a Gentile city. The city was Tarsus. The baby's name? Well, let's join the Jewish godfather as we drop in on his naming ceremony.

A few members of the minyan, a quorum of ten Jewish men, had already gathered at the door. Normally, the woman of a Jewish household would offer warm welcomes to visitors at her door, but the newborn's mother was treated with utmost care during the days following her delivery. Friends and relatives assisted the father in any preparations that had to be made for *Berit Milah*, a tiny infant boy's first initiation into Judaism.

The small house was filled with people. The father, a Pharisee and Roman citizen, was an impressive man. He was one of a few men in the community who seemed to command a certain amount of respect from both Jew and Gentile. When all had finally gathered, the ceremony began. The sandek took his place in a chair next to the father who remained standing. The new father was not a particularly tall man, but the sandek couldn't help but notice that his stature seemed particularly stretched today. And why not? What could make a Jewish man stand taller than a newborn son?

The infant was placed on the sandek's knees, and the father leaned over him with greatest care to oversee the circumcision of his beloved son. He then handed the knife to the mohel, the most upright and expert circumcisor available in Tarsus. The father watched anxiously for the interval between the cutting of the foreskin and its actual removal. He could not help but smile as he competed with his wailing son for the attention of the quorum as he spoke the benediction, "Who hath sanctified us by His commandments and hath commanded us to bring him into the covenant of our father Abraham" (Code, IV, p. 43).

With the exception of the sandek, all who gathered stood for the ceremony and responded to the benediction with the words, "Just as he has been initiated into the covenant, so may he be initiated into the study of the Torah, to his nuptial (marriage) canopy, and to the performance of good deeds" (Code, IV, p. 44).

No one could deny the blessings of good health God had already bestowed on the infant boy. The sandek had to hold him securely between his calloused palms to keep the child from squirming completely off his lap. His tiny face was bloodred, his volume at full scale. This may have been his first bout with anger, but it would not be his last. Had the ceremony not held such sober significance, the sandek might have snickered at the infant's zeal. He did not dare grin, but he might wonder if God would. Tears of joy stung his eyes. The child lying on his lap was yet another piece of tangible evidence that God was faithful to do as He promised. In a society where a child could be discarded as rubbish, nothing was more important to the Jew than offspring. Yes, God had been faithful to a thousand generations.

The circumcision was completed but not soon enough for the master of ceremonies. The sandek cradled the child with a moment's comfort and then handed him to his father whose voice resonated throughout the candlelit home, "His name is Saul!"

As if only a few could hear, the guests rehearsed the words in one another's ears. "His name is Saul! His name is Saul!" A perfectly noble name for a Hebrew boy from the tribe of Benjamin, named for the first king of the chosen nation of Israel. A fine choice met with great approval. While a great feast ensued, the mother slipped the agitated infant from his father's arms and excused herself to nurse the child.

Custom demanded that the father host a feast to the limits of his wealth. A man who offered less than he could afford at his son's circumcision was entirely improper. If baby Saul's father was anything at all, he was painfully proper. Yes, this would indeed be a child well-reared. "I have much to learn from the father of Saul," the sandek surmised.

Darkness was quickly falling when the sandek and his wife finally reached their home. "Dear wife," the sandek thought out loud, "Our Saul seems special, does he not?"

"Dear man," she teased, "he looked like every other

eight-day-old infant boy I've ever seen: mad as a wronged ruler!"

They both laughed heartily. She prepared for bed as he reached for the Torah, trying to fight off the sleep quickly overtaking him. He repeated the words of the Shema; and then he walked over to the mezuzah, fastened to the doorpost of the house, and placed his fingers on it. The mezuzah was a small, longitudinally folded parchment square, containing twenty-two lines, some of the most vital words of God. He responded to the touch with the familiar words of his own father every night of his life, "The Lord is my keeper" (Code, II, p. 62). He crawled into bed, remembered their words, and smiled once again. Then he whispered as his thoughts drifted into the night, "I still say he's special. Full of zeal, he is. Just something about him. . . ." (*To Live Is Christ*, pp. 6–9)

There was something about Saul indeed. He was a little one who was chosen by God.

A friend stood admiring a beautiful tiny baby. As I walked by, I heard him whisper, "It's such a shame they grow up to be people!"

How utterly like God! The great I AM who flung the stars across the sky entrusts His miracles to moms and dads who know nothing about what we're doing. If the plan didn't come from the Wisdom that created the universe, we'd have to question the sense of it all. But somehow we muddle through, and in spite of all our mistakes they do indeed become "people."

Thank goodness, in some of the most important roles we'll ever fill, we're not alone. I wrote the following poem to my dear friend of many years, Johnnie Haines, after our babies graduated the same spring from high school. However poorly or well we'd done that thing called parenting, we'd done it together. After all, what are good friends for?

Side by Side

It's happened, my friend
They're almost grown
Out the door
On their own

Needing us just
As bad as before
Sometimes we'll think
We need them more

Unwelcomed change
Strangely true
This is what
We raised them to do

Empty rooms
Then they'll come home
Friends to see
Talk on the phone

A minute here
A minute there
Still we'll know
We were there . . .

Watching them play
Watching them grow
Breaking up fights
Bandaging toes

From Sunday school
To Mother's Day Out
From kindergarten
To Brownies and Scouts

From Big Wheels
To souped-up cars
From sleeping bags
To football scars

Cried 'til we laughed
Laughed 'til we cried
One moment proud
The next horrified

Dobson's books
On dusty shelves
It's time for them
To try it themselves

Oh, my friend
It's been fun
In many ways
We've just begun

So much ahead
Mothers confide
Let's stick like we started:
Side by Side

❦

My romance with Jesus Christ began in a tiny circle of baby-bear chairs in a Sunday school class of a small-town church. My teachers were not biblical scholars. They were moms and homemakers. I'm not sure they ever delved into the depths of Scripture or researched a single Greek word. They simply taught what they knew. I don't know any other way to explain what happened next: I believed.

I remember thinking how handsome Jesus was in those watercolor pictures and how I had never seen a man with long hair before. I wondered if my daddy, the Army major, would approve. My favorite picture was the familiar one with the children climbing all over Jesus' lap. As I recall, it was the only one I ever saw that captured Him smiling. I determined quickly that big people bored and upset Him and little people made Him quite happy. (*Jesus, the Only and Only,* p. xi)

❦

Watercolor Mister

Watercolor mister
Are you really real?
Can you guess what I'm thinking?
Do you know how measles feel?

And do you mind me asking, Sir
Just how old are you?
That much older than my teacher?
She says she's sixty-two.

Watercolor mister
Do you always smile?
Or do you stick your tongue out
Every little while?

And do you really know that lady
With the jar upon her head?
And does she have a flat top
When she takes it off for bed?

Watercolor mister
I think you look real nice.
So maybe you could give me
A little good advice.

I'm getting pretty tall
But my dad says I'm a pup.
What do you think I should be
One day when I grow up?

Mine.

Yes, His . . .

***

Holding Us

We often see ourselves as fragile, breakable souls.
We live in fear of that which we are certain
we can't survive.
As children of God, we are only as fragile as our
unwillingness to hide our face in Him.
Our pride alone is fragile.
Once its shell is broken and the heart laid bare,
We can sense the caress of God's tender care.
Until then He holds us just the same.

***

Amanda

I always planned to have at least ten children. Soon after we were married, my husband gave me the grave news: He only wanted a couple of children. I was devastated. I immediately retorted with the words, "But we agreed!" He smiled and responded, "No, Honey, you agreed." I have to snicker as I recall wondering if such a blatant omission from our premarital discourses was grounds for an annulment. (I am quite serious.) Little did my husband or I know that I was already expecting child number one.

Finally holding Amanda in our arms had a strange effect on each of us. Keith decided he might just change his mind and want three or four. I, on the other hand, decided maybe I would just have one. Nothing prepared me for the intense sense of vulnerability a seven-pound infant gave me. Someone suddenly had direct, unabashed access to my heart. I was terrified I would lose her. I prayed constantly for God to watch over her, then gripped the rail of her crib and stared at her while she slept just in case He was too busy. Most of the time, I simply held her through her nap time so I could be assured she was OK and in good hands. Reluctantly, I'm sure, God entrusted me with another child, and I set out to drive her almost as crazy as I had my first. (*To Live Is Christ*, pp. 23–24)

Twilight Wishes

Star light, star bright
What name does God call you tonight?
Wish I may, wish I might
Know the One who made the light
And gave the seas their boundaries
And grew bouquets by desert streams
And echoed words in caverns deep
"Let trees applaud and rocks not sleep
And cattle on a thousand hills
Eat from the hand of He who wills
For every nation, tribe, and tongue
To fall before the Risen One
And hail Him as the matchless King
And join hosts as angels sing,Holy, Holy, Holy."

Star light, star bright
Morning Star to God's own right
Wish you may, Wish you might
Come before the dark is light.

Childhood . . . such a precious time of innocence. At least that's the way God intended it to be. But sooner or later childhood gives ways to other paths. Those paths lead us many places. Sometimes they take us to times of sweet fellowship with Christ and with other travelers. Sometimes the path is marked with fruitful service that makes a difference in time and eternity. Sometimes our footsteps trace a descent into the valley of the shadow. But even amid the gloom we can know that following Christ always leads ultimately home.

SHADOW

Have you, as I, sometimes cried out to the Lord over His purpose in pain? Have times of confusion, threat, or loss caused you to petition heaven? Have you believed that to know the why would answer your need? I still lack many of those answers, but of two things I am sure. God is strong, and He is loving (Ps. 62:11–12).

Sometimes we can look back and see that God had a better yes to follow a painful no. In many other cases we simply have to continue trusting God's goodness. In this journey I may have learned little of why God chooses to do as he does, but I have found one way God consistently uses the valley. In the land of the shadow, He teaches us to rely on Him.

I May Never Walk on Water

I may never walk on water,
but I'll never drown.
God may never part the oceans,
but I'll stand my ground.
My faith is not in my beliefs
but in the One I've found.
His word is sure,
when I am not
His heart and mine are bound.

My Name Is Pride

My name is Pride
I cheat you of your God-given destiny . . .
    because you demand your own way.

I cheat you of contentment . . .
    because you "deserve better than this."

I cheat you of knowledge . . .
    because you already know it all.

I cheat you of healing . . .
    because you're too full of me to forgive.

I cheat you of holiness . . .
    because you refuse to admit when you're wrong.

I cheat you of vision . . .
    because you'd rather look in the mirror than
      out a window.

I cheat you of genuine friendship . . .
    because nobody's going to know the real you.

I cheat you of love . . .
    because real romance demands sacrifice.

I cheat you of greatness in Heaven . . .
    because you refuse to wash another's feet
        on earth.

I cheat you of God's glory . . .
    because I convince you to seek your own.

    My name is Pride. I am a cheater.

You like me because you think I'm always looking
        out for you. Untrue.

I'm looking to make a fool of you. God has so much
        for you, I admit, but don't worry

if you stick with me

you'll never know.

We've probably all heard it. "Pride goes before a fall." OK, technically that's not what Proverbs 16:18 actually says. It tells us that "Pride goes before destruction, a haughty spirit before a fall," but the common paraphrase does work. From pride it really isn't far to *had*.

⌖

Had

"My name is Had. You may know me, but you may not know my new name. You may have no idea what I've been through because I do my best to look the same. Oh, I'm scared to death of you. I used to be just like you. I once held my head up high without propping it on my hymnal.

"I was well respected back then. I even respected myself. I was wholeheartedly devoted to God, and if the truth be known, somewhere deep inside I was sometimes the slightest bit proud of my devotion. Then I'd repent because I knew that was wrong, and I didn't want to be wrong. Not ever.

"People looked up to me. And life looked good from up there. I felt good about who I was. That was before I was Had. Strangely, I no longer remember my old name. I just remember I liked it. I liked who I was. I wish I could go back. I wish I'd just wake up. But I fear I'm wide awake. I've had a nightmare. And the nightmare was me. Had.

"If I could really talk to you, if you could really listen, I'd tell you I have no idea how all this happened. Honestly, I was just like you. I didn't plan to be Had. I didn't want to be Had. One day I hadn't, then the next day I had.

"Oh, I know now where I went wrong. I rewound that nightmare a thousand times, stopping it right at the point where I departed the trail of good sense. The way ahead didn't look wrong. It just looked different. Strange, he didn't look like the devil in that original scene. But every time I replayed it, he dropped another piece of his masquerade. When he finally took off his mask, he was laughing at me. Nothing seems funny anymore. I'll never laugh again as long as he's laughing.

"If only I could go back. I would see it this time! I'd walk around the trap camouflaged by the brush, and I would not be Had. I would be Proud. Was that my old name? Proud? I can't even remember who I was anymore. I thought I was Good. Not Proud. But I don't know anymore.

"Would you believe I never heard the trap shut? Too many voices were shouting in my head. I just knew I had got stuck somewhere unfamiliar, and soon I didn't like the scenery anymore. I wanted to go home. My ankle didn't even hurt at first. Not until the infection set in. Then I thought I would die.

"I lay like a whimpering doe while the wolf howled in the darkness. I got scared. I pulled the brush over me and hid. Then I felt like I couldn't breathe. I had to get out of there or I was sure it would kill me. I didn't belong there. I refused to die there.

"I pulled and pulled at that trap, but the foothold wouldn't budge. The blood gushed. I had no way out. I screamed for God. I told Him where I was and the shape I was in. And He came for me.

"The infection is gone. He put something on it and cleaned it up instantly. As He inspected my shattered ankle, I kept waiting for Him to say, 'You deserved this, you know. You've been Had.' Because I did and I know and I have. He hasn't said it yet. I don't know whether He will or not. I don't know how much to trust Him yet. I've never known Him from this side. My leg still hurts. God says it will heal with time. But I fear that I will always walk with a limp.

"You see, I wrestled with the devil, and he gave me a new name. My name is Had."

A Healing Captive

O, God, who frees the captive,
Do not liberate this carnal slave for freedom's sake
For I will surely wing my flight to another thorny land.
Break, instead, each evil bond
And rub my swollen wrists,
Then take me prisoner to Your will
Enslaved in Your safekeeping.

O, God, Who ushers light into the darkness,
Do not release me to the light
To only see myself.
Cast the light of my liberation upon Your face
And be Thou my vision.
Do not hand me over
To the quest of greater knowledge.
Make Your Word a lamp unto my feet
And a light unto my path
And lead me to Your dwelling.

O, God, who lifts the grieving head,
Blow away the ashes
But let Your gentle hand upon my brow
Be my only crown of beauty.
Comfort me so deeply,
My Healer,
That I seek no other comfort.

O, God, who loves the human soul
Too much to let it go,
So thoroughly impose Yourself
Into the heaps and depths of my life
That nothing remains undisturbed.
Plow this life, Lord,
Until everything You overturn
Becomes a fertile soil
Then plant me, O God,
In the vast plain of Your love.
Grow me, strengthen me,
And do not lift Your pressing hand
Until it can boastfully unveil
A display of Your splendor.

Nanny's Box

When I was in the third grade, I had the worst set of buck teeth in the free world. I'm talking terminal buck teeth. (I shared in greater detail in *Things Pondered*.) I took a fall mouth-first when I was about five years old. With mouth wide open, I sailed into the coffee table, shoving my baby teeth against my permanent teeth lodged right behind them. Within a few days my baby teeth turned black. I braced myself for the short wait until they were sure to fall out. And that, they did.

I couldn't wait to get in my new teeth, anticipating how pearly white they'd be after a dreadful mouthful of black. Pearly white they were, but when they grew in, they grew straight out of the front of my gums because my displaced baby teeth had left them there. I need you to picture this. I'm not talking overbite here. I'm talking teeth you could set your sandwich on and save it for later. Are you seeing it?

In those days, for whatever excruciating reason, orthodontists made you live with teeth like that before they would put wires on them and force them into submission. Meanwhile your self-esteem suffered in ways no one with straight teeth can imagine. Certainly, worse things can happen, but the teasing I took during the two years I remained in that dreadful shape affected me for years. The fact is, much worse things had actually

44

happened but they weren't nearly as overt as a mouthful of buck teeth. Factor childhood victimization into the equation, and the figures added up to some serious misery.

The climactic point of my dental crisis came in the third grade with the upcoming annual class pictures. You know, the kind with the blue background. The kind you look back on and ask, "Where was my mother?" and "What idiot let me fix my own hair?" and "What in heaven's name was I wearing?" All of you have a picture like it, so remember you own and add my buck teeth to it. Pretty, isn't it? I announced to my mom, "I'm not having my picture taken. I am absolutely not." Only I didn't say it like that. The unfortunate arrangement of my teeth left me with a decided lisp. I don't doubt I added the word "absolutely" to force a little spit into the pronouncement.

My mother returned, "You most certainly are, young lady. You are so beautiful to us. Anyway, before you know it, we're going to fix those teeth."

I said, "But I'm not going to have my picture taken until we do."

"Oh, yes, you are." In those days I'm not sure I knew I could disobey my mother, especially if she was talking "young lady" talk. She got that look anyway. And who wants to deal with that look? On second thought, how would she like to deal with my look?

I stood in the bathroom at the mirror and practiced trying to simply shut my lips together. My lips had literally not touched since my teeth had grown in fully. My goal was not to look pretty for the picture. It was trying to look normal. I thought if I could cover the hideous things, I'd look like everyone else. No, I wouldn't be able to smile, but perhaps I'd just look like a more serious and mature child. Meditative. Dramatic. Even exotic. Years later people would look at our elementary school yearbook and muse, "We should have all known what a serious thinker she was. Just look at her even then." Yep, that was the plan.

I practiced until my lips were sore. I worked until I finally had a look I thought I could tolerate. At that point in my life, I kept my left hand over my face constantly. (Incidentally, when I'm upset, or when I'm feeling insecure, my family tells me I still tend to put my left hand over my mouth.) During the third grade, I even held my paper down on my desk with my left elbow, held my hand over my mouth, and wrote with my right hand. To any rational thinker, this was no time for a picture, but no mother's love is rational, is it? Neither is their eyesight accurate.

The day came for the pictures. I stood in a long line of third graders with my stomach in a knot. Finally, the school photographer motioned to me and said, "Your turn!" I walked over to the place where "X" marked the spot and stood in front of the camera . . . with my hand over my mouth. The photographer said, "You're going to have to put your hand down, honey."

I asked, "Are you ready to take the picture?"

He said, "Of course."

My retort: "Then count to three." All said with my hand over my face.

He counted, "One, two, three," and I dropped my hand. He took the shot. I put my hand back up and scurried off.

"I did it!" I thought to myself victoriously. I lived through it. "That wasn't so bad, now was it?" I asked myself. And it wasn't until about six weeks later. At the very end of the school day, the teacher pulled out a stack of pictures and placed them with a thump on her desk. Remember the kind with the cellophane window on the front of the picture packs? That's the one. She passed them out one by one, mentioning our names and oohing and aahing sweetly as she set them on each desk. When I realized what was about to happen, my stomach turned with dread. Sure enough, she walked over to my desk totally oblivious to the laughter that was about to break out. She slapped my picture packet down right in front of me, face up.

No one had time to see it because I fell over it immediately. No matter. They pretended they did. In my memory it sounded like a thousand kids roared with laughter, but I'm quite certain as an adult that it was only a few. You know, if I hadn't hidden my mouth all the time, they would not have been so anxious to see it. It's the age-old game of hide-and-seek. Anything we try to hide, someone else will try to seek. Back in the third grade I had some very sweet classmates, too, but somehow we have a hard time making out encouragement in the roar of meanness, don't we? Some of my classmates began to make fun of me and call me by names that weren't new to me.

I was devastated. And on second thought, I was furious. It's always more convenient when you have someone to blame for your humiliation. A certain someone who called me "young lady" came to my mind instantly. I cried all the way home that day, and when I reached my house, I stomped straight into the kitchen where my mother and grandmother were sipping their instant Folgers. I yelled as angrily as I could, "Don't you ever make me do anything like that again!" I took those school pictures, ripped them to shreds, and threw them in the trash. I accomplished just what I intended. I made them feel as badly as I felt. Of course, now I wish I hadn't, but at the time I was a spout waiting to spew. Years passed and when the last orthodontist bill was paid, I'd worn some kind of wire on my teeth for twelve solid years. (I still have a retainer.) That's how long it took to fix those teeth. (My mouth has been a lifelong challenge for God to fix.)

My precious grandmother, whom I called Nanny, passed away when I was sixteen years old. Bless Dad, she had lived with my parents since they married, so you can imagine how much her constant presence was missed. I was in my early twenties one day when I was visiting my mom at my parent's home. She said, "You're not going to believe what I found the other day." She got down a box with a lid on it. On the outside of it the words "Nanny's Keepsakes" were written in marker in my grandmother's own handwriting. It was the most wonderful discovery.

I asked, "Where has this been?"

Mom explained that she's found it in the attic in search of something else. When Nanny knew her days were few, she apparently boxed up some treasures she'd kept for decades so they'd all be in one place. She probably put it in her closet, and after she died, my mother gathered up all her things that weren't suitable for Goodwill and put them in the attic. I'm sure Mom didn't have the heart to look through them closely at the time. When she stumbled on the box in the attic years later, she'd forgotten it even existed.

"I've not had a chance to really look through it. I've just taken the top off. Let's you and I take a look," Mom said. It was just like finding a royal box of buried treasure. Inside was my grandfather's bookkeeping ledger. He was a lawyer during the Great Depression. I was so intrigued by the kinds of things he recorded as his payment for services. On many of the spaces for payments received, he'd written "the eggs or the ham." No charge. On the box were letters my Nanny's sons had written her while overseas in World War II. Precious things. Priceless things. Things that defined her better than any written biography ever could. I found her Bible, marked with her own red pen. For the length of time I shared a feather bed with her, I remember a rare night when I didn't go to sleep with her reading God's Word right next to me.

I could not believe what treasures were spread before us from the box marked "Nanny's Keepsakes." I pulled every iten out one by one and studied them carefully. Thinking I'd surveyed everything in the box, I started to tuck the keepsakes back in their places when I caught a glimpse of a thin white envelope wedged in the corner. I picked it up, and the weightlessness of it made me assume it was empty. However, it was clearly sealed.

I asked my mom if she knew what it was.

"I have no idea, honey."

"Well, I wonder if we should open it?"

She said, "I'd say Nanny's not going to. If you want to know what's in it, you're going to have to open it yourself."

I slipped my finger through the buckled edge very carefully. I couldn't help but imagine my grandmother licking the seal and sliding her index finger across the envelope to make sure it was closed. When I'd opened it, it appeared empty so I shrugged with disappointment and said to my mom, "There's nothing in it." Then something caught my eye. In the corner of the envelope was a torn piece of an old picture. I pulled it out, and to my total astonishment it was a piece of a picture of a little buck-toothed girl in the third grade.

I can only assume that my grandmother had pulled that picture out of the trash, sealed it in an envelope, and put it in a safe place. When she gathered her treasures, somehow she placed it among them. I looked at my mother, tears streaming down my cheeks, and cried, "Why did she do that?" Nanny loved all of her grandchildren. She did not love me more than any of the rest. I could not imagine why she'd thought to do such a thing.

Mom honestly didn't know. Neither did I for many years. In retrospect, however, I think I've figured it out. The answer is hope. Pure, biblical, life-sustaining, gloriously unreasonable hope. Everything is possible for him who believes, our Savior said. Though I believe my grandmother suspected something was amiss with me, I don't think she knew I'd ever been victimized. In reality, my severe overbite was the least of my problems. All she probably knew was that I was a troubled child, scared of her own shadow, quick to tears and, in her estimation, sweet and gentle. After all, for too short a time I was the only one of her grandchildren that had actually been her roommate. I believe my grandmother pulled out that picture, prayed over me, sealed me in an envelope, and said something like, "I will never see what you do with this life, but I can hope." (*Jesus, the One and Only*, session 10) Yes, you can hope.

❦

Come, Captive, Free!

Help me, Lord, I cry aloud
To foreign masters I have bowed
The cheater of Your grace to me
Still holds me in captivity.

Old chains so long around me bound
Their clanging ceased to make a sound
Bruised and bleeding at Your Throne
From casting self-inflicted stones

"Guilty once and guilty twice!"
The adversary grips the vice
Shoulders weary from the shame
Fiery darts—easy aim.

I'm ready, Lord, I'm at the end
Crushed beneath the yoke of sin
Believing lies he told to me
When all along, I'd been set free.

Let me see him dip the bread
Who kisses me 'til captive led
Unmask to me the Judas sin
That masquerades as my good friend.

Then keep my heart exposed to light
'Til every sin is in my sight
And quick confessed before he brings
His accusations to the King.

In hopelessness don't let me wait
To be set free at Glory's gate
A victor once, a victor twice
'Til victory is a way of life.

A son of glory, child of grace
To one day meet You face-to-face
And hear You say, "Come captive free!
My willing slave of liberty!"

A Tattletale

I told on you to God today
A mouthful's what I had to say
About the way you've treated me
And in plain sight for all to see!
Don't think you've gotten by with this
I took Him quite a detailed list
You can bet you'll hear from Him
He'll get you back! So until then . . .
Expect a blessing.

FELLOWSHIP

The journey with Christ certainly includes the valley of the shadow. Fortunately, two wonderful facts more than offset this somber truth. One is the fact that we also sometimes get to tread the high places with Christ. The other is the fellowship with both Christ and His servants as we tread this road together. Let's contemplate the sweetness of sitting long in His presence.

Sitting Long

Have you waited long upon the Lord?
For His Word? For His hand?
Until He speaks
Until He acts
. . . and He surely will . . .
You need not wait upon His love
Patience to wait does not come from
suffering long for what we lack
but from sitting long in what we have.

Audience of One

The more I wait on the Lord, the more I come to realize what's really important in life. Nothing compares with time spent enjoying God's presence. So may I tell you one of my fondest memories ever of time spent with the Master? The setting was Greece. We were in Athens taping the video sessions for *Beloved Disciple*. I'll just pick the story up there, just the way I read it to the ladies gathered in Athens.

"Yesterday I performed a ballet in my hotel room just for God. Yep, complete with pointed toes, leaps, twirls, backleans, and pliés. Admittedly, I was a little scared I might throw my back out on the leans. My knees also creaked just a tad on the pliés, but actually it was quite beautiful. I only know that because that's what I felt like I heard Him say at the end when I appropriately went to my knees and threw my hands back behind me for a dramatic conclusion. I don't know if I got a standing ovation or not. It's so hard to see those kinds of things from here. I'm also not sure if He applauded. I couldn't hear for the sobs. My own, not His. I know that's what you were thinking.

"Oh, I'm sorry. I've caused some of you the discomfort of being embarrassed for me. Oh, please, don't be. Save it for times I get far more undignified than that. Anyway, I'm sanguine enough to believe that just below the surface of your embarrassment for me, you are just the teensiest bit jealous. As long as no one can read your thoughts, could you admit you sure wish you knew how to dance the ballet? Who said I know how? I haven't had a lesson since childhood when I quit because I was the worst one in the class. I don't know how to sing, either, but that doesn't keep me from bellowing my lungs dry!

"Actually, I know about jealousy. It's one of my least favorite feelings, but I felt it just recently. One of my co-workers was called by God to a thirty-day fast of juice and water, so she could binge on Him. Never one to want to be left out, I told her that I had asked God to tell me some way I could also observe a fast of sorts in support of her during her thirty days. I did. He turned me down flat. I have had the humiliation of sitting at the same lunch table with her for twelve days at work, while I ate like a glutton and she drank her clear broth. And secretly, I feared she was his favorite. Don't get me wrong. I want her to be His favorite, just like I want you to be His favorite. I just want to be His favorite, too. And somehow I thought He couldn't approve of my fajitas and salsa as much as He approved of her broth.

"I hugged my coworkers tightly and said good-bye a week ago and left them to come all the way to the other side of the world for this taping. I miss home. And I miss work immensely. But to be honest, I had also looked so forward to being with God all alone. Two nights ago I ordered room service. A really wonderful meal. A filet cooked to medium perfection with flamed brandy sauce. Don't worry. They say the alcohol cooks right out. I don't know, though. I did feel a little woozy afterwards. A baked potato and sour cream. Lots of bread and butter. And I paused to bless the food. Oh, I didn't close my eyes or anything. We do that for others, not for God. I told Him how thankful I was to have a date with Him and eat the meal all alone with Him. Then I sopped the first bite in the sauce. Then I remembered my coworker and felt another twinge of guilt—a condemning lesser spirituality. I wondered, *Would God bless this taping more if I fasted?*

"Then I realized that God is where He calls us. Whether we are feasting and going to the ballet, or fasting and going to the desert. Do you know what? Just then when I wrote the word *desert*, I accidentally typed in an extra *s* and spelled *dessert*! That's me! I suppose I'll die trying to find the desserts in my desert, and don't tell me there's no such thing! I have yet to come out of the desert without some kind of dessert. Granted, sometimes I ate a lot of locusts before the honey ever came, but came it finally did! If one of these days you happen to look down at my cold, hard body in a casket, my only hope is that I'll still have chocolate all over my mouth! Glory! Now don't let me confuse you here. You may have to be called to a fast, but you never have to wait to be called to the ballet. You can dance anytime, even in the desert—oops! I almost wrote *dessert* again! Maybe that was it all along. The dance in the desert is the dessert.

"What? What did you ask? Oh, what song did I perform?

"Yesterday in my room—ah. A slaying arrangement of 'Be Thou My Vision.'

'Be Thou my vision, O Lord of my heart;
Naught be all else to me, save that Thou art;
Thou my best thought, by day or by night;
Waking or sleeping, Thy presence my light.

'Be Thou my wisdom, and Thou my true word;
I ever with Thee and Thou with me, Lord;
Thou my great Father, I Thy true son;
Thou in me dwelling, and I with Thee one.

'Riches I heed not, nor man's empty praise;
Thou mind inheritance, now and always;
Thou and Thou only, first in my heart;
High King of heaven, my treasure Thou art.

'High King of heaven, my victory won;
May I reach heaven's joys, O bright heav'n's Sun!
Heart of my own heart, whatever befall;
Still be my vision, O Ruler of all.'

"Well! I'm so relieved. Some of you that looked pretty embarrassed for me earlier look a little less horrified now. Thank goodness. I really don't set out to make sure people know I'm weird. I like for people to like me. I just want to make sure they really know who they think they like. I played like someone others might like too long. Still, if you like me again, I think I'll stop while I'm

61

ahead, and not tell you about the peppier song I put on next when I then slid to the music with my socks on the marble entryway in my hotel. If you're new to this, please don't try that at home. Whatever you do, start with the ballet. After all, sliding in your socks comes with a little maturity. Amen?"

You may think I have something for dancing. That's not true. I do love dancing before the Lord, but I also love to put on a nice powerful, powerful Steve Green song and grab a pencil and act like I'm the conductor and conduct the entire side of the CD. Why? Because I think it makes God laugh. I think He thinks it's funny. And I think He's a blast! Yes, life is sometimes so hard we can barely stand it, but we stand it because He's wonderful! Oh, that He would be our laughter! Our joy! Deeper than our depths! The culmination of everything of our heart's deepest desire! (*Beloved Disciple*, Introduction Session)

The River of Mercy

There is a river of mercy
Just beyond the pride
Down the street from secrecy
Around the bend from lies.

No signs that say "No Trespassing"
No need to sneak in fear
Turn right beyond the marker saying,
"Bring your trespass here."

The waters there are brisk and clear;
The bank is never steep.
Quick waters smooth the pebbles clean
So enter with bare feet.

I'll meet you in that river
If you'll come with no disguise.
Bring to me your honesty
And let the waters rise.

They'll cover every guilty stain
And rinse away each sin.
Splash in my refreshment, Child,
Go ahead! Dive in!

There is a river of mercy
Come and freely swim
My Son is waiting at the gate
And He'll escort you in.

The Streets of Jerusalem

David danced down the streets of Jerusalem when he finally became the king God promised he would be. I may be rushing ahead to our final installment on the road home, but at this point my thoughts turn to the man after God's heart as he finally traveled home.

That day there just might be one who can't seem to stop singing. Oh, yes, I believe David will dance once more down the streets of Jerusalem—this time without an eye to despise him. Oblivious to anyone but God, the focus of his affections, the passion of his heart. David will dance his way to that same familiar throne, but this time it will be occupied by Another. No one above Him. None beside Him. David will see the Lord high and lifted up, and His train will fill the temple. He'll fall before the One who sits upon the throne, take the crown from his own head, and cast it at His feet. He'll lift his eyes to the King of all kings, and with the passions of an entire nation gathered in one heart, he will cry, "Worthy!"

Surely God the Father will look with great affection upon the pair.

All wrongs made right. All faith now sight.
He'll search the soul of a shepherd boy once more
And perhaps He will remark
How very much he has
A heart like His.

River of Delights

I want to drink from your river of delights.
> I want to dance before Your throne.
I want to chase You to the depths and the heights.
> I want to live all my way home.

I want my eyes to be open till they're closed,
> and faith gives way to that holy sight.
But while I've the dust of Earth between my toes,
> I want to live with all Your might.

I want to shout hallelujah while I can,
> living life in the abundant and beyond.
Splashing in Your Spirit and lifting up my hands,
> I want peace like a river, not a pond.

I want to drink from Your river of delights.
> I want to dance before Your throne.
I want to chase You to the depths and to the heights.
> I want to live all my way home.

(*When Godly People Do Ungodly Thing,* session 3)

Fragile

We often see ourselves as fragile, breakable souls.
We live in fear of that which we are certain
we can't survive.
As children of God, we are only as fragile as our
unwillingness to bend the knee.
Our pride alone is fragile.
Once its shell is broken and the heart laid bare,
we can sense the caress of God's tender care.
Until then He holds us just the same.

The Sinner's Prayer

During the videotaping of *Jesus, the One and Only,* God spoke to me clearly about doing something I had never done on videotape before. He told me to lead the group in a prayer, that is, in one sense, the first prayer God will ever hear from a person. By that I mean the prayer confessing sin and accepting Christ's gift of eternal life—the sinner's prayer.

Of course I know that God hears everyone's prayers. And sometimes in His infinite grace He answers those prayers. But a line separates the unbelieving world from God's children. That line somehow involves our willingness to bow the knee to Christ and receive His forgiveness.

No single sinner's prayer exists. The simplest appears in Luke 18:13 "'God, have mercy on me, a sinner.'" I have to grin as I tell you that my version is longer than most sinner's prayers, but you would find that to be a very natural thing coming from me. I'm wordier than everybody else you know. But I want to make sure we have covered all the bases!

Even more than the rest of this journey, I wish I could be there to hold your hand and pray together. I want to ask three kinds of people to pray this prayer. If you are in Christ and you know you have deliberately received Him into your life, then I'm going to ask you to pray it in remembrance of Him. You see, every single year, that's what the Jews did; they recounted the faithfulness of God through the Passover. They still do. He honors that. So I invite you to pray remembering and celebrating the fact that Christ lives in you.

You are the second type person I want to pray for and lead in prayer if you think maybe you've received Christ as your Savior but you're not really sure. You've gone for years not having a full assurance. Do you remember that Hebrews 10:22 bids us "draw near to God with a sincere heart in full assurance of faith"? It says Christ died on that cross for you to have a full assurance of your salvation. You're not absolutely positive? Then do it today. Nail it down as clearly as Christ was nailed to that cross.

The third possibility is if you have never deliberately invited Christ Jesus into your life. I want you to know something. It would be the honor of my entire life to lead you in this prayer. If I have ever known anything to be truth, I have known that there is truth in the plan of salvation. So I'm going to ask you to repeat these words after me in prayer.

Most Holy God, I am so aware of my own unholiness.

I confess to You, I am hopeless and helpless under the weight of my own sin.

I confess I am a sinner in desperate need of grace.

I acknowledge that Jesus is Your Son.

He came to this Earth as the perfect Lamb of God.

He was nailed to a cross for me.

He knew me before time began.

He took on all my sins in advance—past, present, and future.

His death paid the penalty for every sin I would commit.

This moment, I receive Your Son, Jesus Christ, into my life by faith.

Just as He rose on the third day, raise up His resurrection life in me this moment.

Holy Spirit, I welcome you.

Come into my heart to stay.

My life is signed and sealed until I am safely delivered into Your heavenly kingdom.

Most Holy God, Sovereign Creator of the universe, I now call You, Father.

My Abba, my Dad. For I have been saved by the blood of the Lamb.

My life is now sacred, no longer common or unclean.

From this day forward I belong to You.

Help me to live in gratitude for so great a salvation.

For Thine is the kingdom, the power, and the glory forever and ever.

In Jesus' blessed name. Amen.

Blessed Anonymity

There is a name above all names—
Let mine be lost in His.
Hide me in His crimson heart,
O secret way of bliss.

Blessed anonymity,
Count my life but loss.
Jesus, the One and Only,
Tread over me dear cross.

One life alone worth finding
Nail mine unto the tree.
Till Jesus ever shining
Is all beheld in me.

Bring Him forth each day I live
And leave me in the tomb.
I see no other glory
Make not the smallest room.

An Unfamiliar Place

I'm in an unfamiliar place
No homey comforts here
Not sure of where I'm going
Not sure what brought me here.

The light is dim, my way obscured
Dark shadows jump and scare
A soundless voice then whispers deep,
"Walk on! I'll meet you there."

A lamp illuminates my feet
Just one step at a time
The voice cries out, "Forsake your plans—
Possess this land of mine!"

Trembling still, I walk along
The path secured for me
At last my eyes behold the land,
But I glance back to see.

There were no shadows there at all
No monsters over me
'Twas rivers parted all along
'Twas waves held back for me!

I'm in an unfamiliar place
Peculiar comforts here
No turning back, my homesick soul
His will is home for thee.

—Joshua 3

SERVICE

We've been sojourning in the land of fellowship, but it's a twin kind of place. True camaraderie has a way of leading to the land where servants toil. What could compare with the heart shaing between Christ's early servants who spent long days on the trail together?

Acts 17 describes Paul's trip with his companion Silas from Philippi to Thessalonica. They traveled one hundred miles without the benefit of a motorized vehicle. Then when persecution followed the missionaries, the Christians in Thessalonica got Paul out of jail and sent them off to Berea. Having narrowly escaped the Thessalonians in the night, the tenacious missionaries traveled approximately fifty miles to Berea. Imagine the discussions that must have passed between two such servants of Christ. Surely the fellowship would be more than worth the aching muscles at the end of the day. Surely such brotherhood echoes the love between Christ and His disciples.

Who Is This?

I thought I knew Him, after all
I'd walked with Him for years.
I'd heard Him laugh until He cried
I'd seen His human tears.

We'd race each other to the shore
And soak our callused feet.
Miles of road behind us
I'd watch Him fall asleep.

Sure, I saw such miracles
Astounding as they were
In hopes that He was one of us
I'd think what I preferred.

I guess I wanted to believe Him
Less so I could stand
To walk beside Him with my pride
To know Him man to man.

But just as I'd grow easy
With what I thought I knew,
The winds would rise to differ
And the skies made black of blue.

Fear came to overtake us
As He slumbered over there
We were sure that we would drown
We charged He did not care.

I expected Him to take control
His strong arm to the oar
To steer us on to safety
To get us to the shore.

But in a thousand thoughts I never
Dreamed of what we got
This crew of unbelieving
This foolish, selfish lot

Saw Him rise up to His feet
As if on solid ground
Give one rebuke and instantly
The storm came tumbling down.

Then those who claimed to know Him best
Knew Him not at all.
We grew more frightened of this One
Than of the windy squall.

Who is this One that winds obey
And waves become as glass,
While mortal creatures carry on
As if He's not? I ask.

I guess I wanted to believe Him
Less so I could stand
To walk beside Him with my pride
To know Him man to man.

He looked so very like us,
But be very sure, He's not.
Somehow, some way He was a man
While being very God.

At times He seemed just like a friend,
Unique but one of us.
Then suddenly we saw the One
Who formed us from the dust.

Who is this One that winds obey
And waves become as glass
While mortal creatures carry on
As if He's not? I ask.

I guess He wants us to believe Him
More so we can stand
To walk beside Him on the seas
To know Him God to man.

To fear Him more than we fear life
While safe beneath His care
Then ask again, "Who is this One
I thought I knew somewhere?"

The One and Only of His kind
We know Him not at all
Oh, for grace to see the One
Who makes glass from the squall.

The intersection of fellowship with Christ and toil together in His service drives me to press on. Unfortunately, I cannot help but contrast the sacrificial service on the pages of Scripture with the halfhearted and self-conscious worship we casually serve up to God. Does the following convict you as it has me?

A House that Grace Built

I took my seat one Sunday
On my favorite pew
Got comfy on a cushion
With a perfect view.

I could see the Robinsons
They're on the rocks, it's true.
The Jones were there—their boy drinks
The Smiths—they just got sued.

And there was old man Worthington
More money than the bank
But I've watched very carefully
He never fills the plate.

The organist filled up her pipes
We stood to sing a hymn
I nudged a friend beside me
"Look what the cat dragged in!"

"How dare he darken sacred doors
Some nerve to walk in here."
My nose rose up to greet him
Made sure he saw me sneer.

The perfect conversation piece
He was at lunch that day
We only stopped long enough
To bless the food and pray.

That night I crawled into my bed
I tossed and turned 'til late
I reach for my antacids
"Must be something that I ate."

I fell into a restless sleep
And had a dream so real
I stood before a mansion
In a crimson field.

I reached my hand to knock
On a door shaped like a cross
My eyes fell on a message
There on the door embossed.

This is a house that grace built
You are welcome here
You'll find no condemnation
Enter without fear.

The door opened before me
I found myself inside
It felt so unfamiliar
I found no place to hide.

Suddenly before me
Were faces that I knew
The Robinsons, the Smiths, the Jones
Just to name a few.

And there was old man Worthington
Passing 'round a plate
Filled with appetizers
Many took and ate.

A gentle hand slipped into mine
He gave me quite a fright
It was that man the cat dragged in!
But no cat was found in sight.

"So glad you graced our sacred door,"
He said, "Feel right at home"
Then all rose up to greet me . . .
If I had only known.

Though he looked a little different
No doubt it was that Man
But when He put His arms around me
I saw nail scars in His hand.

Unlovely

Until we have loved the unlovely,
The Father's heart has never beat within us.
We are left here to love.
All that we do void of abandoned charity
Is dust in the bottom of an empty chalice.
The new wine of Christ's love
Is never sweeter than when the chalice is lifted
To the Father to be filled . . .
That the unlovely might drink.

Have you joined us for the study of Paul the apostle? The Lord impressed me to end *To Live Is Christ* with these lines that seemed to me to summarize the heart of a servant who poured himself out to reach the unlovely.

Drink Offering

Most Worthy Lord,
make me a drink offering
and take me not home
until the cup is overturned
the glass broken
and every drop loosed
for Your glory.

(Last line of *To Live Is Christ*)

⚬━━┿━━⚬

Your People

Oh, Lord,
we are Your People.
We do not yet begin to fathom
our desperate need of You; for indeed until we
are free, we are helpless to realize the depth of our
bondage. We come before You in confession this day.
We confess to You that we have not misunderstood
Your command
to love one another. We confess to a willful disobedience
and to an
inner slothfulness that sees a true heart change as
simply too much
trouble. We confess that we have reduced Your "new
commandment" to a
"new consideration." A warm and fuzzy—though highly
unattainable—fairy
tale. Our hearts are held fast in the vice grip of self-
centeredness. We confess to
You this day, Lord: our love is small. Our hearts are not
dwarfed by the evil one;
rather by our own fists. We have stomped our feet
before You as spoiled children,
crying, "Mine!" We confess the sin of our preference for
a privy few. And we confess that we have not cheated

others of our love nearly as much as we have cheated
ourselves of the privilege to love them. And finally,
Lord, we confess our disbelief.
We do not believe You are greater than our hearts. Holy
Father, some of us today,
with fear and an inner war of selfishness raging, are
willing to hold out our fists
to You. Tucked pitifully within You will find our small
hearts. If we will but
choose to take the fisted hand we hide behind our back
and extend it to You,
You will graciously peel away each finger until we are
released. Oh, come
Glorious Liberty! Free us to love as we've been loved,
for only then
will we truly live. Surround me with those so different
from me.
Let me not continue on in the gripping constraint of
self-centeredness. Take my crumpled heart and inflate it
until it begs to burst with the warm blood of
Your Son. I choose this day to love.

Make me a vessel.
In the liberating
name of Jesus,
Amen.

I thought I might share with you a simple story of something I experienced recently. It's not really profound. And certainly not prolific. But it caused me to think . . . and appreciate. May God make it a blessing.

○═◆═○

Need Me

It was my first Saturday off in a good long while. Lots to do. I was invited to a birthday party. "Sorry, wish I could come. But my parents need me today." A concert at church. "Better not. My parents need me today." A good movie. "Love to—next chance I get. But my parents really need me today." This was a day for proper priorities. I headed to the hospital to take care of my mom while Dad was in surgery. Every slowpoke this side of the Pecos pulled out in front of me. I weaved in and out of traffic then came to a screeching halt. In typical Houston style, six lanes of freeway merged into two due to endless road construction. I sat impatiently. "Hurry! My parents really need me today."

I finally whipped into the parking lot, grabbed my purse and ran toward the hospital. I pushed the up button on the elevator; it crept like a child's Christmas. "Come on! My parents really need me today." Then the long awaited ding. "Finally!" I flew to the waiting room. My heart raced. I hurried to the desk. Gave them my name. "I'm Mr. and Mrs. Green's daughter. My mom needs me today. I'm not sure where she is." The attendant handed me a note: "Hi Sweetie! We're in the cafeteria. Dad's already been taken in." I ran back to the elevator, pushed down, and waited for another ding. I hopped off and ran through a maze of halls with arrows leading to the cafeteria. Every step of the way, I could feel fresh gray hairs sprout from my scalp. "Of all days to be late, Beth. She really needed you today."

I played bumper cars with every human being in the cafeteria. "Excuse me. Pardon me, please." Finally I saw a silver-haired woman at a table. She looked so frail. She's been through so much. She really needs me today. Suddenly she looked up and saw me . . . youngest daughter. Kid number four. She grinned ear to ear and said, "Get yourself over here. Are you hungry?"

"No ma'am. Not really. My stomach's a little upset."

"Get you a dessert," she said. "You're too skinny. Here's some money."

So she pulled out her wallet, extracted a few dollars, and handed them to me. My big sister sat close by, borrowing our mom's same infectious grin.

"Actually, Mom," I said, "I ran out the door without grabbing any cash. I think I will get something to eat if that's OK."

She got me up to speed on Dad as we walked back to the waiting room. She, my sister, and I then passed the time with what this world is coming to. Finally they called mom back to post-op. We jumped up too.

"Sorry ladies," the nurse said. "Just your mom."

But our parents need us today, I thought.

Mom laughed, searched her purse, and said, "Now girls, where'd I put your daddy's teeth?"

She disappeared down the hall digging in every pocket for an extra set of choppers. Several minutes later, Mom peeked through the doors mischievously. "Come on, girls. Come see your daddy."

We finally got him home. I ran to get his prescription. I asked how long it would be. "Just a few minutes ma'am." Good. My parents really need me today. I sped back to the house. We fixed Dad a comfortable nest. We propped him up with feather pillows. My sister said she needed to get back to her little ones. Mine are older. I'll stay. Mom and Dad really need me today.

Dad began to rest, and I asked, "What shall I get us for supper, Mom? Shall I order a pizza?" She jumped up contentedly and said, "I think I have a few things right here." (Mom has always had an uncanny way of cooking something from nothing. We've often said she should write a book called *A Hundred and One Meals without Ever Going to the Grocery Store*.) She threw together the best meal I'm quite sure I've ever eaten. We sat at the kitchen bar on stools and ate . . . talking about my teenage girls and the ones she used to have. We talked about sons, and we talked about broken hearts when things sometimes don't turn out the way we planned. We talked about how you live through things you think you can't. We laughed over the same salt and pepper shakers we had when I was little. The pepper shaker hadn't had a working hole in it since at least 1971. You still have to take off the lid and pinch it with your fingers—then try to keep from sneezing all over the table. We talked about our common love for Christ, and tears welled up in our eyes over His faithfulness. I still had a Sunday school lesson to prepare for the next morning. I used Daddy's books and commentaries. He still prepares every Sunday even though he's retired from teaching—just in case someone might be out.

Dad began to squirm. Mom had been instructed to get up with him every two hours. They really need me tonight. I should spend the night. I ran all the way home and grabbed my things. By the time I returned, it was practically bedtime. I brushed my teeth, and I could hear mom rustling around in my bedroom. When I came in, she was gone—but my bed was turned down. My eyes moved from the bed to the walls. My brothers', sisters' and my baby pictures were all in frames close by those of our own children. I glanced back at the den and then the kitchen. Warm colors. Familiar sights and sweet smells. A simple home. Simple people, really. Never made much. Never lacked much. But they were a success. They have survived life without having grown cold or cynical. Their kids turned out just fine, and their grandkids adore them.

They weren't perfect. They weren't famous. They were just plain good.

My mom interrupted my thoughts by saying, "Honey, you know about that awful mattress."

"I love that mattress, Mom."

As I climbed into that familiar bed in my parents' home, I wasn't sure the last time I ever felt so loved . . . or felt life was so bearable. I fluffed my pillow. Pulled my covers over me. Contented tears washed my cheeks, and I whispered, "Thank you, God. I really needed them today."

Lord, Make Me a Student

Not of higher learning but of Your higher ways,
not to expand my mind but so my heart will change.
Give me the courage to withhold
nothing from You worthy of a lesson.
Your Word as my text,
each circumstance Your pen,
my heart as Your page . . .

Take my needs and teach me Dependency.
Take my failures and teach me Grace.
Take my pain and teach me Compassion.
Take my fears and teach me Faith.
Take my waits and teach me Patience.
Take my storms and teach me Trust.
Take my tongue and teach me Reverence.
Take my deserts and teach me Thirst.

Lord, make me a student,
never let me cease growing.
For as long as I can see my reflection in the mirror
I am not yet complete.

Lord, make me a student
and take me not home,
until You look in my face
and see the reflection of Your own.

❦

Lesson with a Hairbrush

If I've learned anything at all, I've learned that our God is practical. In one of the video sessions for the Bible study *A Heart Like His,* I shared a story that illustrated God's immense practicality to me, and I suppose I've been asked to repeat this story as often as any I've ever told. I'm humbled that God granted me an experience and life lesson that has somehow touched other hearts as deeply as it touched mine. Over and over I've noticed that God will teach us something in His Word, and then He'll show it to us in the world. That's exactly what He did on this occasion.

I was heading to the east coast, and I had a layover in Knoxville. I was going from a rather large airplane to a very small plane, so I joined other travelers in one large room with several doors leading to commuter aircraft. Wanting to make good use of an hour layover, I sat with my Bible on my lap and continued to work on memorizing the first chapter of John. Incidentally, I know no better way to memorize Scripture than on an airplane. If you can't memorize well, you need to fly. You just read a small portion of Scripture out loud a number of times then look out the window of the plane and try to say it from memory. I don't know why it works so well. Perhaps being up in the air is more conducive to higher thoughts. You'll have to try it for yourself. I'll warn you, however, you may or may not prove a blessing to the person sitting next to you. At one point on the plane ride to Knoxville, I got stumped on the next word, and the woman sitting beside me filled it in for me. And she didn't appear blessed.

Back to the layover. I had the Bible on my lap and was very intent upon what I was doing. I'd had a marvelous morning with the Lord. I say that because I want to tell you that sometimes it's a scary thing to have the Spirit of God really working in you. You could end up doing some things you never would have done otherwise. Life in the Spirit can be dangerous for a thousand reasons not the least of which is your ego.

Seventy or eighty of us filled this commuter area of the Knoxville airport, all waiting to board our planes. The seating in this large room had us facing one another in various rows of vinyl chairs. I see that peculiar arrangement often in airports, but I've never been able to figure it out. Certainly, I am a people watcher, but I prefer to do my people watching a little less conspicuously.

All at once the people sitting across from me were captivated by a sight over my shoulder. I smoothed down my hair, thinking my Texas-do may have been a bit much for them. In Texas we tend to believe the higher the hair, the closer to God, but I've noticed that other regions in the nation may not have reached such deep revelation. Since their expressions didn't change after I called my hair into submission, I knew something was going on behind my back. From the look of their expressions, I could also tell it was horrifying. I wanted to look so badly, but Southern girls who mind their manners know you can't stare while everyone else is staring. You wait to stare until all the others have stopped.

I tried as hard as I could to keep my eyes on my Bible, but I was so distracted by my fellow travelers that I couldn't concentrate. I had no idea what was going on back there, but I knew it had to be something big. In just a few minutes, I could see activity over my left shoulder, and finally I glanced out of the corner of my eye. I will never forget what I saw. An airline hostess was pushing a wheelchair with an old man who looked not a day younger than 127 years old. I've never in my whole life seen a human being look that old and that weary and that drawn. I tried to keep from staring, but he was such a strange sight. Humped over in a wheelchair, he was skin and bones dressed in clothes that obviously fit when he was at least twenty pounds heavier. His knees protruded from his trousers, and his shoulders looked like the coat hanger was still in his shirt. His hands looked like tangled masses of veins and bones. The strangest part of him was his hair and nails. Stringy grey hair hung well over his shoulders and down part of his back. His fingernails were long. Clean. Unpainted, thankfully, but strangely out of place on an old man.

I looked back down at my Bible as fast as I could, discomfort burning my face. As I tried to imagine what his story might have been, I found myself wondering if I'd just had a Howard Hughes sighting. Then again, I'd read somewhere that he was dead. So this man in the airport . . . an impersonator maybe? Was a camera on us somewhere? I recall being on an airplane on my way to Memphis once with a planeful of Elvis impersonators. Unbeknown to me, it was the king of rock and roll's birthday. I'd never seen so many men with bigger hair than mine or such a penchant for talking in lyrics. OK, don't be cruel. The point is, the strange old man could have been an act, I supposed. But if he was, he deserved an Oscar. And a new makeup artist.

There I sat trying to concentrate on the Word to keep from being concerned about a thin slice of humanity served on a wheelchair only a few seats from me. All the while my heart was growing more and more overwhelmed with feeling toward him. Let's admit it. Curiosity is a heap more comfortable than true concern, and suddenly I was awash with aching emotion for this bizarre-looking old man.

I had walked with God long enough to see the handwriting on the wall. I've learned that when I begin to feel what God feels, something so contrary to my natural feelings, something dramatic is bound to happen. And it may be embarrassing. I immediately began to resist because I could feel God working on my spirit and moving me toward the man. I started arguing with God in my mind, *Oh no, God, please no.* I looked up at the ceiling as if I could stare straight through it into heaven and said silently, "Please, Lord, I know what's going on here. You want me to witness to this man. God, please don't make me witness to this man. Not right here and now. Please! I'll do anything. Put me on the same place with him. I'll witness to him on the plane, but don't make me get up here and witness to this man in front of this gawking audience. Please, Lord!"

Don't get me wrong. I don't have a problem with sharing the gospel with someone. I love to share Jesus, but this was a very peculiar-looking man in a setting that seemed a bit unconducive to spiritual awakening. I tried my hardest to continue my memory work when I felt a serious rebuke from God. Something like, "Hide my Word in your heart. Don't hide in my Word from your heart." His Word is meant to teach us how to love Him and love others. To use the study of God's Word as an

99

excuse not to serve is like using food as an excuse not to eat.

Then I heard His commanding voice loud and clear. When I say God spoke to me, it wasn't an audible voice. Like most of you, I would have instantly morphed into a corpse. Rather, a very clear statement entered my mind that I knew wasn't my own thought or imagination. In my experience, I usually know God is speaking by three conditions.

First of all, what I believe I "heard" has to be consistent with His Word. God never speaks contrary to Scripture. The character of God expressed in the whole counsel of His Word is how we know, for instance, that God never tells mothers to kill their children no matter how a tormented woman may insist He has.

Second, what I believe I "heard" sometimes seems to come somewhere out of left field, and I know I wasn't even on that same intellectual track at that moment. In other words, it wasn't me, and it is consistent with God.

Third, I am far more likely to discern the voice of God accurately if I'm in the Spirit. I don't mean something mystical by being "in the Spirit." I'm talking about being in close fellowship with God with my sins freshly confessed and the fruit of the Spirit infiltrating my own. When I'm in a spiritual condition to really listen and He's speaking something clearly consistent with His Word but quite different from my own thoughts, I usually think,

That's got to be God. Sometimes I'm off base. This wasn't one of those times.

There I sat in the blue vinyl chair begging His Highness, "Please don't make me witness to this man. Lord, please, please! Not now! I'll do it on the plane if you'll put us on the same plane." Then I heard it: "Oh, I don't want you to witness to him, I want you to brush his hair."

The words were so clear, my heart leapt into my throat, and my thoughts spun like a top. My chin practically dropped to the ground with shock as I quickly surveyed the two prospects. Do I witness to the man or brush his hair? No brainer. I looked straight back up at the ceiling and said, "God, as I live and breathe, I want you to know I am ready to witness to this man. I'm on this, Lord. I'm your girl! You've never seen a woman witness to a man faster in your life! What difference does it make if his hair is a mess if he is not redeemed? I'm on him. I'm going to witness to this man!"

Again as clearly as I've ever heard an audible word, God seemed to write this statement across the wall of my mind: "That's not what I said, Beth. I don't want you to witness to him. I want you to go brush his hair."

I looked up at God and quipped, "I don't have a hairbrush. It's in my suitcase on the plane, for crying out loud! How am I suppose to brush his hair without a hairbrush?" Where I come from, you fix your hair, spray it stiff, and don't touch it again until bedtime. Clearly this wasn't bedtime. God was so insistent that I almost involuntarily began walking toward the man as these thoughts came to me from God's Word: "I will thoroughly finish you unto all good works" (2 Tim. 3:7 KJV). I stumbled over to the wheelchair thinking I could use one myself. Even as I retell this story to you, my pulse has quickened, and I can feel those same butterflies. I knelt down in front of the man and asked as demurely as possible, "Sir, may I have the pleasure of brushing your hair?"

He looked back up at me and said, "What'd you say?"

"May I have the pleasure of brushing your hair?" To which he responded at volume ten, "Little lady, if you expect me to hear you, you're going to have to talk louder than that." At this point I took a deep breath and blurted out, "SIR," (No, I'm not exaggerating) "MAY I HAVE THE PLEASURE OF BRUSHING YOUR HAIR?" At which point every eye in the place darted right at me. I was the only thing in the room more peculiar than old Mr. Longlocks. Face crimson and forehead breaking out in a sweat, I watched him look up at me with absolute shock on his face and say, "If you really want to."

Are you kidding? Of course I didn't want to! But God didn't seem interested in my personal preferences right about then. He pressed on my heart until I could utter the words, "Yes, sir, I would be so pleased. But I have one little problem. I don't have a hairbrush."

"I have one in my bag," he responded. I went around the back of that wheelchair, and I got down on my hands and knees. I unzipped the stranger's old carry-on hardly believing what I was doing. I lifted out undershirts, pajamas, and shorts until I finally came to the bottom of the bag. There my fingers wrapped around the familiar bristles of a brush. I stood up and I started brushing the old man's hair. It was perfectly clean, but it was tangled and matted. I don't do many things well, but I must admit I've had notable experience untangling knotted hair mothering two little girls. Like I'd done with either Amanda or Melissa in such a condition, I began brushing at the very bottom of the strands, remembering to take my time and be careful not to pull. A miraculous thing happened to me as I started brushing that old man's hair. Everybody else in the room disappeared. There was no one alive for those moments except that old man and me. I brushed and I brushed and I brushed until every tangle was out of that hair. I know this sounds so strange but I've never felt that kind of love for another soul in my entire life. I believe with all my heart, I—for that few minutes—felt a portion of the very love of God. That He had overtaken my heart for that little while like someone renting a room and making Himself at home for a short while. The emotions were so strong and so pure that I knew they had to be God's.

His hair was finally as soft and smooth as an infant's. I slipped the brush back in the bag, went around the chair to face him. I got back down on my knees, put my hands on his knees, and said, "Sir, do you know Jesus?"

He said, "Yes, I do." Well, that figures. He explained, "I've known Him since I married my bride. She wouldn't marry me until I got to know the Savior." He said, "You see, the problem is, I haven't seen my bride in months. I've had open-heart surgery, and she's been too ill to come see me. I was sitting here thinking to myself, *What a mess I must be for my bride.*"

Only God knows how often He allows us to be part of a divine moment when we're completely unaware of the significance. This, on the other hand, was one of those rare encounters when I knew God had intervened in details only He could have known. It was a God moment, and I'll never forget it. Our time came to board, and sadly we were not on the same plane. Oh, how I wished we had been. I was deeply ashamed of how I'd acted earlier and would have been so proud and pleased to have accompanied him on that aircraft. The airline hostess came to get him, and we said our good-byes, and she rolled him on the plane.

I still had a few minutes, and as I gathered my things to board, she returned from the corridor, tears streaming down her cheeks. She said, "That old man's sitting on the plane, sobbing. Why did you do that?" She insisted, "What made you do that?"

I said, "Do you know Jesus? He can be the bossiest thing!" And we got to share. I learned something about God that day I'll never forget. He knows if you're exhausted because you're hungry, you're serving in the wrong place, or it's time to move on but you feel too responsible to budge. He knows if you're hurting or feeling rejected. He knows if you're sick or drowning under a wave of temptation. Or He knows if you just need your hair brushed. God knows your need. He sees you as an individual. Tell Him your need.

I got on my own flight, sobs choking my throat, wondering how many opportunities just like that one I had missed along the way . . . all because I didn't want people to think I was strange. God didn't send me to that old man. He sent that old man to me.

Think Bigger, Boys

Think bigger, boys!

You've yet to find I've got all the power all of the time.

Think bigger, boys!

While it is day, watch what I do, do what I say.

Think bigger, boys!

See every scene with Me in the middle, reigning as King.

Think bigger, boys!

For one day you'll see Me in My glory, then you'll say to Me,

"We should have thought bigger."

Could we end our journey through the land of service with a commission to faith? This public declaration came from the online study *Believing God*. Our Bible study group in Houston led women around the world as we declared our intention to be believing servants marked by obedient faith. If you care to join our number, I'd love to count you among my friends who have made this pledge. Would you verbally declare your faith? And could we help one another to remain faithful to it?

Commission to Faith

Lord, today I accept my calling.

 Not to perfection or performance.

My calling is to faith.

 I have been chosen for this generation.

I have a place in the heritage of faith.

 I'm going to stop wishing and whining.

I'm going to start believing and receiving.

 What Your Word says is mine.

I won't let others steal my hope.

 I will not argue with the Pharisee.

I will believe, and therefore speak.

 For You, my God, are huge.

Nothing is too hard for You.

 Our world needs Your wonders, Lord.

Rise up from Your throne, O God.

 Renew Your works in our day.

I confess the unbelief of my generation.

 And I ask You to begin Your revival of faith.

In my own heart.

 For You are who You say You are.

 You can do what You say You can do.

 I am who You say I am.

 I can do all things through Christ.

 Your Word is alive and active in me.

Enemy, hear me clearly.

My Father is the Maker of heaven and earth.
And you are under my feet.

Because for today and the rest of my days.
I'm believing God!

THE ROAD HOME

———

As we near the end of any journey together, I find myself flooded with bittersweet feelings. I feel a sweet sensation, for I'm amazed and honored that you would choose to spend your time with this woman. The bitterness comes with parting yet again. If I had my way, we'd have unlimited time for me to hear your story. But as we begin the last leg of our travel together, we can do it with celebration. The road home beckons. It calls to every servant of Christ who has shared the imperfect fellowship of this land of shadows. Oh the joy of that land where you and I will have all the eternity to share our hearts as we take in the infinite wonders of our Christ.

My heart almost leaps from my chest at the thought. So as you begin this final phase of our journey, brew yourself a cup of tea. I'll grab a tall dark-roast coffee. Let's contemplate that day when the Father will welcome us home for good.

My Prodigal

I'll run to you when skies aren't blue
And life has let you down
When you've lost hope—the will to cope
And rainbows seem to frown
When childhood dreams are lost in streams
Of steady woes and noes
When fairy tales are scary veils
Of families turned to foes
When you set out to end self doubt
And end up more confused
When messes made are hands you played
And there is no excuse
When all you planned has turned to sand
Mirages disappeared
When giving up's the only cup
To wash away your fears
When nothing's left—no promise kept
But one I made to you
And in the distance I can sense you
Take a step or two
With open arms—a cloak from harms

Pace quickened like a youth's
I'll sing,
"My child's come home again!"
And I will run to you!

⊙━━◆━━⊙

Elohim

He is Elohim, Creator,
    the Omnipotent who rules.
He's the Sovereign King of glory
    and Earth is His footstool.

He is the Alpha and Omega,
    the beginning and the end.
He sends forth lightning
    that later checks back in with Him.

He speaks worlds into existence
    and spins them out in space.
He gives orders to the morning
    and shows the dawn its place.

He prophesies the future,
　　then orders it fulfilled,
He bears fruit from a landscape
　　that man has never tilled.

He feeds the beasts of the field
　　from the palm of His hand;
He watches while they bear their young,
　　then teaches them to stand.

He gives the seas their boundaries
　　and hides His creatures deep;
He teaches eagles how to fly
　　and nest upon the steep.

He makes the clouds His chariot
　　and rides on wings of wind;
He champions the victim
　　and brings proud men to end.

He is Immanuel, God with us,
　　come to earth through Christ;
He's the kinsman Redeemer
　　who paid the slave man's price.

He's King of kings, Lord of lords,
　　and worthy is the Lamb;
He holds the keys to life eternal,
　　where the dead in Christ now stand.

He's enthroned between the cherubim,
    and great is His reward,
The devil His defeated foe,
    the weapon His swift sword.

The story has a moral,
    so I'll hasten lest you tire,
Whoever you perceived He is,
    you might aim a little higher.
    (*Believing God*, sesson 2)

Consume Me, O Lord

Consume me, O Lord,
Flood my soul with your Son.
Leave nothing uncovered,
Leave nothing undone.

Set me on fire,
Consume all my dross.
Make beauty from ashes
And gain from my loss.

Consume me, O Lord,
Be the life in my bones.
Put your head in my marrow
Till Jesus alone.

Can set me aflame
With Your holy fire
Unquenchable passion
Exquisite desire.

Thrill all my senses
With sacred romance;
Consume me, O Lord,
Come bid me to dance.

Down streets paved in gold
A pure virgin bride
Nothing to run from
Nothing to hide.

Consume me, O Lord.

Footsteps to Follow

Few in our time have embodied the consumed life better than Bill Bright. He truly has left footsteps we ought to aspire to follow. Bill recently met his Savior face-to-face and what a reward he must have received. Watching the ministry of Campus Crusade for Christ for a number of years, I observed how Bill was somehow able to stay on in interdenominational work, ministering to and with believers from a range of backgrounds. I've watched, and I've wanted in some ways—ways that God would have me in my own personal ministry—to imitate some of the markings that made such ministry possible for him.

For many, many years, I wished I could interview him in some way, but of course, that was not possible. Strangely enough, a couple of weeks before God took him to glory, I received a call from his office and spoke with him on the phone. I said, "I've always wanted to ask you a question. I too have been called to stand on the interdenominational bridge that you have stood on for such a long time. I've seen that most people go to one extreme or another, and I want to stay right there. How did you do it? What would you tell me? What advice would you give me?"

I could tell he was laboring to breathe, with the disease that he had been bearing for so many months and years. He took a deep breath and said, "Beth, love, love, love. And when you are tired of loving, you love some more. When you don't agree with them, you keep loving some more. And when you really don't agree with them, you love them even more. You just continue to love, love. Make the mark of your life love—that when you die, they will say, 'Didn't she love?' Make it love. Make it all about love."

Is love your priority? The fruit of the Spirit is love at work, home, church, and in life.

The Apple of Your Eye

Lord, I want to be the apple of Your eye,
The joy of Your morning, the rainbow in Your sky—
The culmination of Your creativity,
One among the few who dares to set You free.

To occupy a heart and teach it higher ways
To introduce eternity to souls in human clay.
I want to make You smile, I want to make You laugh,
I want to make You nudge Your Son
—and nod—and then perhaps . . .

I'd give You just a taste of what You've given me:
Delight so indescribable, Love's sweet liberty—
You are my One and Only, my hope can rest assured
My wagon's safely hitched, my rocky path secured.

You are my yesterday—
You are my by and by,
No need to doubt this moment . . .
I'm the apple of Your eye.

"Keep me as the apple of your eye." (Ps. 17:8)

Wedding Portrait

And speaking of the apple of God's eye, may I tell you an earthly story that, at least for me, sheds light on a heavenly relationship? I told this story in the forward of *Breaking Free,* but here I'm going to relate it as I told our gathered Bible study group in Athens for the taping of *Beloved Disciple.*

As I was preparing for my husband's and my twentieth wedding anniversary, for the life of me I could not think of what I wanted to get him. He's a very sentimental man. You have to get him something sentimental because if he can afford it, he already owns anything he wants. You understand? And most of your men are like that too. They're hard to buy for.

So I just said, "God, you need to tell me what I can get my man. I need a really great idea." As I continued to bring the request before God's throne, He began making a suggestion to my heart, with a stir at first. He started bringing back to my mind the early part of my marriage and the pain of my wedding day. It was an extremely hard day for me. I don't know how to explain it to you. I didn't understand it until many, many years later. I was feeling so much shame on my wedding day. It was a day I was supposed to feel beautiful. And I did not feel beautiful.

I felt like a fraud though I honestly wasn't one. I had gone to a lot of trouble to make absolutely sure that

I had an off-white dress instead of a white dress because I did not want to be a lie. Some of you know all too well exactly what I'm talking about. Shame is a horrible feeling. When you love God and want to please Him, yet you are too bound in terrible shame to believe wonderful things of Him. You've made so many mistakes, and try as you may, you can't take them back. Nothing about that day seemed beautiful to me. We have a picture the next day as we depart for our honeymoon, and I felt wonderful that day. But on my wedding day, walking down that aisle, the day of a little girl's dreams come true was a nightmare for me. The whole ceremony is a blur.

I had pictured, when I was a little girl, that I would have a huge wedding portrait to hang over our blazing fireplace. Well, all we had was a heater in the bathroom, and a picture certainly didn't seem fitting over the toilet. I didn't have money enough for a photographer, so I just spent the bare minimum to have some memento of the day. I didn't even buy my dress. I rented it to save money. Simply said, this was not the kind of wedding day we all pictured as little girls. As I was contemplating the gift for Keith, those memories were still painful to me.

Purposely the Lord began to prick that painful memory. Though the enemy brings up difficult memories just to hurt us, God never does. When God reminds us of something painful, He has one purpose: to bring us healing. As I fought back the tears over those old memories,

I wondered where on earth they were coming from after all these years. Then I felt as if God said to my aching heart, "You know, Beth, you never did get that picture made."

"What picture?"

"That wedding portrait."

"Well, it is a little too late!"

"Who said?"

And the Lord planted the idea for the perfect anniversary gift on my heart. He seemed to say, "My darling, we have done so much work. I have restored you. It is time for you to see yourself restored. It is time for you to put on a white wedding gown and get your picture taken for your husband."

I called a friend of mine who's a makeup artist in Houston, a godly, godly young woman. I know her so well that I knew she would have a fit of praise. She squealed on the phone, jumping up and down until I had to yell to get her attention. "You can't tell anyone, Shannon. This is our secret."

Beside herself she responded, "I'll set up everything. You just show up when and where I tell you. I'll take it from there."

So that's exactly what I did. She hid me in a room at a photography studio where I couldn't see what she was doing. She wouldn't let me near a mirror as she prepared me for my portrait. She presented me with a beautiful, wedding dress, sparkling white from head to toe, slipped it on me and zipped it up. If fit perfectly . . . just like Cinderella's shoe. Ah, Cinderella. We've all wanted to be her, haven't we? Shannon carefully applied my makeup, swooped my hair up into a twist, and put on my veil. Then she guided me carefully through the doors until we came into a room with a large, full-length mirror.

I hardly recognized myself. I do believe it was the prettiest I've ever felt in my life, and you know as well as I do, every little girl wants to grow up to have her own Cinderella moment. The photographer was so tender that his eyes filled with tears. "I've just got to be honest with you," he explained. "I've never taken a picture of a bride this old." Realizing his faux pas, he quickly said, "Now that's that's not what I mean. I mean one that's been married for so long." I was his only forty-one-year-old bride that had been married for twenty years.

The weeks dragged by until I finally got a call from the photographer that the proofs were ready. I chose what I believed would be Keith's favorite, had it enlarged into a twenty- by twenty-four-inch portrait and bought the most ornate (OK, gawdy) gold frame you can imagine. I also had smaller ones made for each of my daughters. I wrote a letter to all three of them explaining what the picture meant to me.

I could hardly wait for the night of our twentieth anniversary. I asked the girls to hang around until I presented Keith with his gift because I had something for each of them as well. And they all read their letters at the same time. My husband is all man. Add rugged to tall, dark, and handsome, and you've got the Texan I married. He read the letter, folded it back up, dropped his head in his large hands, and began to sob. I knew he would. That he's man enough to cry is one of the things I love best about him.

Keith stood up with the oversized portrait of his forty-one-year-old bride, and he began walking all over the house. He would stop at one place, hold the picture up to the wall, and shake his head no. Then he's stop at another and shake his head no again. Finally he walked right over to a focal point in our den and stared at a pre-mium spot on the wall. The girls and I simultaneously caught our breath because we could hardly believe what he appeared to be considering. He set the picture down. He took a deep breath, tears streaming down his checks. I thought, *He's crying over the deer.* He hung that pic-ture up right on the very same nail, and it hangs there today.

He stepped back, stared at the picture, face wet with tears, and said, "That is the trophy of my life." That is a restored bride. You know, one of the tragedies of silently suffering through destructive, despairing feelings is that you are left to think you're the only one who has ever felt that way. I so deeply regretted not hanging on to my virginity, but then again I'm not sure I really remember when I lost it. I know that even as a very young child I bore a deep sense of shame. I never recall ever feeling anything remotely like purity. In an emotional sense, I never had the chance to feel virginal then I lived out my adolescense according to that self-defeated belief system. I have learned that God's way is always right. His commands are for our sakes and for our freedom. He does not tell us to wait for marriage to have physical intimacy to punish us or to chain us but because He knows the kind of hurt and regret that results when we give something so valuable as ourselves away cheaply and tentatively.

As I've shared my story about the portrait, I've been shocked by the very visible reactions I've gotten from women in the audience. Tears—even grief—have shown on a surprising number of faces from teenage girls to senior adult women who carry deep regrets about the loss of their virginity. I want others who have made the same mistakes or suffered similar victimization to discover what I have. God really can restore honest-to-goodness purity (1 John 1:9). If I may be so bold, God can restore *virginity*, at least spiritually speaking and, I believe emotionally and mentally as well. Didn't the apostle Paul tell the church at Corinth that he wanted them presented to Christ as virgins (2 Cor. 11:2–3)? And hadn't many of them dealt with sexual misconduct and committed sexual sin? Like me, perhaps you repented of sin and even finally came to a place to believe God had forgiven you for the sin, but have you allowed Him to fully restore you? You haven't unless you've come to see yourself as pure and lovely in Him.

Some months ago a precious young woman named Tammie called me and asked me if I would think she was copying me if she had a wedding portrait made like I did. Her story was similar to mine, and she, too, felt impure when she married. God had done an amazing work in her life and her marriage, and she wanted to capture His mercy and grace through a picture in a white wedding dress. I was ecstatic. I even supplied the dress. You see, Beloved, I didn't originate the concept. God did. All we have to do is believe Him.

My dear Tammie wasn't the only one. She just happened to have been one I knew personally, and a framed picture of her in my oldest daughter's white wedding dress sits in my office. In her beautiful hands is a Bible. She wanted to show that she had decided to take God at His Word. I've received a number of letters along the way from women who have decided to act on their belief in a similar way. Is there a way you feel led to act on your belief in God's restored power? Yours may be a different kind of demonstation all together but one that means as much to you. Dear One, believe God and act on it. Few things will ever mean more.

Blessed Condescension

Is it not enough,
Unhidden One,
When seeking
To have found You?
Has my hand yet room
For more than Yours
When bound in knots
Around You?

O, Blessed Condescension!
Willing, Reaching God!

What kind of souls,
O, wretched man,
Have unbridled we?
To require promise
Of reward
For having sought, Lord, Thee?

Mingled here
My shameful lusts
With Heaven's shameless love

My head cast on
Your bleeding Hand
O, God, Thou art enough!

Give, O Giver,
For You must
Give all You have to me
But give Your best
Starve these lusts
Give Thy Son to me.

One day when I was studying, I came upon something that deeply stirred my heart and my imagination.

Ephesians 2:10 tells us, "For we are God's workmanship."

The original Greek word is *poieme* which is translated in English:

Poem.

The Poet

You are the Poet, I am the poem.
You gather my lines from sunshine and storm

Glimpses of faith, steadfast and still
To harrowing falls and stubborn self-will

Dances down Jerusalem streets
To despair beneath the weeping tree

Sometimes pleasure—sometimes pain
Sometimes they blend 'til they seem the same

Each passage of life a poignant phrase
Challenging sense in a senseless maze

Alas, and at the end of time
Rhythm will come and words will rhyme

Paper yellowed, wrestled, and worn
Still You are my Poet . . . and I am Your poem.

John, the Beloved

My eyes grow dim.
My strength grows faint.
I wonder, Lord,
why do You wait?

That day with John
when You walked past,
I was so young—
could follow fast!

We lived, it seemed,
at whirlwind's pace.
Whirling wonders
place to place.

So far removed,
sometimes I dream
I'm there again,
so real it seems.

I laugh with You.
I see You walk.
On waters mad
I hear You talk.

I lean against
Your shoulder there.

I hear You breathe
away my cares.

Dream's rooster crows.
I jerk to wake.
Tears stain my face.
Why do You wait?

My thunder's gone.
The young have come
their place to take
and fast to run.

My passions stilled,
I have no taste
for all but You.
Why do You wait?
My skin wraps bone.
My bones, they ache.
I reach for You!
Why do You wait?

An answer comes,
though none can hear.
While old man weeps,
the Lamb draws near.

"Son of Thunder,
if You knew
hell's angry rumble
over You!

My faithful son,
'tis easier still
to jump the cliff
than climb the hill.

You stayed the course
when days wore on.
Love burned white hot
while life grew long.

Long after faith
of friends sparked sight,
And victor's crowns
replaced their plight,

Yet you remained
and loved again.
Why do I wait,
My faithful friend?

Because the sight
prepared for you
Is beyond white
and beyond blue.

I dim your eyes
Like stage grows dark.
Anticipate!
Till curtains part."

The old man sobbed,
heard not a word,
rose from rock bed,
pained joints stirred.

"Let's see," he mused,
"What day is this?
Ah, Sabbath's past.
Lord's Day it is."

He groaned deep prayers.
He thundered praise.
A man in Spirit
on his Lord's Day.

Then startling came
A voice behind,
like trumpet talking,
voice divine!

John whirled around,
and there He was:
the One who is,
the One who was.

His body froze,
his soul afret.
A sight too much,
he fell as dead.

Then healing voice
spoke life to lung,
"Take scroll and write
the vision, Son.

Am I not still
the God of time?
Make I mistakes?
Have I no mind?

If sovereign I
should choose to wait,
while you yet live—
anticipate!"

Prepare, O bride.
Let eyes grow dim.
Die, lesser sights.
Cast eyes on Him.

Spend yourself
till stage is set.
Beloved Disciple,
love still yet.

What Kind of God Are You?

What kind of God are You, Oh Lord
Perfect Judge, with tongue of sword
Lifted high while hosts bow down
Lightning flashing, rainbow round

What kind of God are You, Oh Lord
That You would leave throne thus adored
Descend to earth, despised of men
Rejected to redeem from sin

What kind of God are You, Oh Lord
Wretched men like me restored
Abyss once bound by wage of death
Killed by Your cross, raised by Your breath

What kind of God are You, Oh Lord
That You would do again the more
Move heaven and earth my heart pursued
Til You who loved, I would love too.

What kind of God are You?

Shining Like the Son

I want to share an imaginative look at something in our future. When I first wrote this a couple of years ago, I really thought I understood from Revelation 19 that the wedding supper would precede His second coming. But now that I look at the text, I'm not sure of that. It could be that it comes after the second coming. The context doesn't tell us for sure. I wrote this with the first understanding. Anyway it's just a fictional writing, so don't take it as interpretation. I pray that it blesses you as we try to picture to the best of our imagination.

Never in the history of heaven or earth had there been such festivities. Unimaginable flowers of textures and colors no human eye has ever seen crowned each table. The smell of food permeated the banquet hall. Bread of heaven, freshly baked. Ladles of honey, creamery butter. Fruits and vegetables unique to the menus of heaven. Goblets of silver and gold filled with the fruit of the vine. The Groom had not lifted His cup since He gathered with His beloved twelve in the upper room. A dozen-less-one who gathered around His table that fateful night had, brief centuries later, turned into ten thousand upon ten thousand.

John the Baptizer stood to his feet as the friend of the bridegroom and offered the toast, "To the Lamb of God, who took away the sins of the world, and to His beautiful virgin bride." "Hallelujah, our Lord reigns!" the crowd responded, as all held up the cup of gathering and drank. Laugher and joyous fellowship filled the hall, new saints celebrated with the old. Peter and John inseparable as usual laughed with Spurgeon, Tozer, and Chambers. Paul set back and smiled like a father as Timothy captivated all of his table with the old, old stories. Corrie was there. Close by were those who had met the Savior in her prison camp. They were now covered with garments of salvation and ate to their fill. Amy Carmichael broke bread and passed generous portions around her table as beautiful brown, Indian hands reached out to receive. Zacchaeus, who had only seen slices of life from the branch of a tree, asked endless questions of a man named Graham, who had traveled the seven seas.

Instruments played the songs of the ages with glorious fanfare. Many danced with tambourines. Voices sang in seven-part harmony. The Groom sat at the head of the table captivated by His bride. As He talked to each person, He touched and gave them His utmost attention. Intently listening to a story passionately told, His concentration was broken by the overwhelming sense that His Father's eyes were on Him. He squeezed the hand of the one testifying as if to explain His change in focus. Then He turned His face toward His Father's throne. No words were necessary. He knew what His expression meant. The Groom nodded and gazed upon His bride.

The sound of His chair sliding back on the floor silenced every voice in heaven. The angels froze. The guests shuddered. The bride's eyes grew wide. Nobody moved but the Groom. He rose to His feet. As if suddenly awakened from a trance, an order of angels disappeared from sight, returning seconds later with countless crowns. No one moved, yet all could see. The royal vestiges were visible from every angle of the hall. Yet when the order of angels had placed the final crown upon His head, they stepped back while saints caught their breath. Though the crowns were many, they wrapped around His head as one diadem. All dominion belonged to the Lamb on His throne.

From the distance came a faint sound. Difficult at first to distinguish, finally it neared until the sound of rhythmic hoofbeats became evident. Only the Groom was standing, but each saint sat tall and strained to see. Gabriel led the most magnificent beast ever created to His rider. His coat was white with a luster like pearls. His mane was strands of gold. His eyes were like wine. His muscles ridged under his coat displaying his immense condition. The Groom stared at him with approval, then smiled with familiarity as His hand stroked his mighty neck.

Two cherubim brought forth a wooden chest laden with gold and brilliant jewels. Saints covered their eyes from the blinding light as they lifted the lid. The dazzling radiance was veiled as they brought forth a crimson robe from within and placed it upon the Groom's shoulders.

The servants tied gold tassels around His neck, and the seraph spread forth His train. From the robe the words blazed forth embroidered in deep purple, "King of kings and Lord of lords."

A royal foot went in the stirrup as Faithful and True mounted His horse. The beast dipped his head as if to bow then lifted it with an inexpressible assumption of responsibility. The Groom gently tugged the reigns to the right, and the animal turned with exemplary obedience. No one moved. No one spoke. No one took their eyes off the rider on the white horse. All stood ready, backs to their audience, waiting.

Suddenly, a sound erupted like rolling thunder. The earth rumbled beneath their feet. Every saint could feel the echo in his heart of the pounding like a thousand tympanis. The Groom released their gaze as the walls of the banquet hall gave way with a stunning thud. Encircling them were horses no man could count, winged, and ready for flight.

The four creatures: one with a face like a lion, one with a face like an ox, one with a face of a man, and one with the face like a flying eagle, flew over the heads of the saints and sang the anthem, "All rise!" Each saint, dressed in white linen, rose from his chair and boarded his horse. The attentions of every saint were quickened by the Groom. His back still turned. His horse made ready. Suddenly, a vapor seeped from the ground and covered the hooves of the horse of Faithful and True. As the vapor rose to His thighs, the fog became a cloud enveloping the Rider inch by inch. Brilliance overtook Him, and He became as radiant as the sun. So great was His glory, the cloud rose to His shoulders and covered His head to shield the eyes of the saints.

The familiar surroundings of heaven suddenly faded, and the sky appeared under His feet. A deafening sound emitted from the middle of heaven like the slow rending of a heavy veil. The sky beneath their feet rolled by like a scroll, and the inhabitants of heaven found themselves suspended in the earth's atmosphere. The planet was their destiny. The Groom was their cue. The cloudy pillar that enveloped Him would plot their course. With swiftness the cloud descended toward the earth. The horses behind Him kept perfect cadence. The earth grew larger as they made their final approach. As they approached, oceans could be distinguished from the nations. The earth turned until Jerusalem faced upward. The cloudy pillar circled widely to the right for the Rider's eastward arrival.

The sun interrupted night as it rose upon the city of Zion and awakened every inhabitant in the land. Rays pouring through their windows were unlike those of any other morning. All who saw it sensed the imposing arrival of the supernatural. The wicked inhabitants of Jerusalem's houses, those who forced the people of God from their homes, shielded their eyes as they filled the city streets. All of Israel was awakened, and the valleys were filled with people gazing upward as much as their vision would permit to something awesomely beyond terrestrial.

Emaciated humans filtered one by one from every cave and crevice—those who had not taken the mark of the beast. Their eyes attempted to adjust to such sudden and abnormal gusts of light after hiding in the darkness for so long. Every eye looked upon the amazing cloudy pillar as it made its approach just east of the city of Zion. The cloud stopped midair.

Suddenly the divine veil began to roll upward inch by inch exposing first only the hooves of the great white horse, then the feet of the Rider. They looked like burning brass in the stirrups. Little by little His crimson robe appeared until it seemed to blanket the sky. His name ascended above all names. The cloud lifted above His shoulder and the knowledge of God was unveiled in the face of Jesus Christ. His eyes burned like fire into every heart.

Those who had taken the mark of the beast ran for their lives, shoving the people of God out of their way, as they took cover in the caves that had so recently sheltered God's faithful. The people of God's covenant and those who had come to their aid remained in the light entranced by the glorious sight. Moaning filled the air.

The Rider on the white horse dismounted His beast. His feet touched down on the Mount of Olives, and the earth quaked with indescribable force. All who were hiding lost their cover.

The large brown eyes of one small boy remained fixed

upon the sight. The whiteness of his teeth contrasted with the filth covering his face as he broke into an inexperienced smile. He reached over and took his mother's bony hands from her face and held them gently. With the innocence, only one sight could possible restore, he spoke, "Look, Mom, no more crying. Surely that is our God. We trusted in Him and He saved us." Even so Lord Jesus come quickly. (*Beloved Disciple*, session 10)

RESOURCES

Believing God. Workbook study published in 2003 by LifeWay Christian Resources in Nashville, TN.

Beloved Disciple. Workbook study published in 2002 by LifeWay Christian Resources in Nashville, TN.

Jesus, the One and Only. Workbook study published in 2000 by LifeWay Christian Resources in Nashville, TN.

Jesus, the Only and Only. Trade book published in 2002 by Broadman & Holman Publishers in Nashville, TN.

To Live Is Christ. Trade book published in 2001 by Broadman & Holman Publishers in Nashville, TN.

When Godly People Do Ungodly Things. Workbook study published in 2003 by LifeWay Christian Resources in Nashville, TN.